Go Seek!

Written by: Nicole & Gregory Elz

Go Seek! A great activity for the entire family to do together. Spending time with family is the most important thing.

Baby Llama asks Mama Llama to play hide and seek!
"Mommy Mommy go seek!" says the Baby Llama.

"Okay you go count to five!" says Mama Llama with a giggle, and off she goes with a wiggle.

Baby Llama counts
" **1,2,3,4,5!** "
and off she goes with a cute little stride.

Baby Llama looks and looks.
Maybe Mama is behind all those books.

Mama, are you over there with the hare?

Baby Llama takes a peek
Where'd my mommy go seek?

Bunny pops out from the little book house,
with no Mama Llama, just a tiny little mouse.

They run to get their glasses off the shelf, then the bunny asks, "How 'bout some more help?"

"Sure," says the Baby Llama! Let's go seek!"
and they hop towards the unicorn stable to take a quick peek.

The friends look and look around the farm
Maybe we need a lucky charm?

Unicorn! have you seen my Mommy?

"No Mama Llama isn't over here

but let's go seek," he yells with a cheer!

"Sure," says the Baby Llama! Let's go seek!"

The friends keep on striding.

Where could Mama Llama be hiding?

Mommmmy...

where are you?! Sings Baby Llama
as the three friends walk the farm.
Do you think she could be hiding behind the barn?

"Look over there!" says the bunny with glee.
Baby Llama sees Mama Llama
hiding behind the honey.

"Found you!" screams Baby Llama.
"You found me!" smiles Mama Llama.

"...with a little help from my friends."
Let's go play go seek again!

The end.

CPSIA information can be obtained
at www.ICGtesting.com
Printed in the USA
LVHW071826190723
752911LV00019B/225